Also by Vera Pavlova

Album for the Young (and Old)

Album for the Young (and Old)

Vera Pavlova

Translated from the Russian by Steven Seymour

Alfred A. Knopf
New York
2017

THIS IS A BORZOI BOOK
PUBLISHED BY ALFRED A. KNOPF

www.aaknopf.com

"[Remember]" first appeared in the *Times Literary Supplement.*

Library of Congress Cataloging-in-Publication Data
Names: Pavlova, Vera (Vera Anatol'evna), author. | Seymour,
Steven, translator.
Title: Album for the young (and old) / by Vera Pavlova; translated
from the Russian by Steven Seymour.
Description: New York : Alfred A. Knopf, 2017. | "Borzoi book"—
Title page verso.
Identifiers: LCCN 2016036395 (print) | LCCN 2016041146 (ebook) |
ISBN 9780451494788 (hardcover) | ISBN 9780451494795 (ebook)
Subjects: LCSH: Pavlova, Vera (Vera Anatol'evna)—Translations
into English.
Classification: LCC PG3485.A875 A2 2017 (print) | LCC PG3485.A875
(ebook) | DDC 891.71/5—DC23
LC record available at https://lccn.loc.gov/2016036395

Jacket illustration by Lisa Pavlova
Jacket design by Janet Hansen

Manufactured in the United States of America
First Edition

for Steve, in loving memory

Contents

I

II

I

Tchaikovsky's *Album for the Young*

Morning Prayer

A rubber dinghy with a fresh patch on the hull;
Grandpa rowing, me and the gudgeons at the stern.
How goes it, live bait, still alive all right?
Two lines cast by the bank, where the current is swift.
Dead bait on the surface, live bait down deep.
Poems are but snapshots taken in dreams.
Honest, I do not miss my childhood, cross my heart.
I wonder if my childhood misses me, if only a bit.

*

A Winter Morning

A blizzard is no problem,
so long as the snow sticks.
I was doing Chekhov,
got Gogol instead.
Mom was doing someone's head,
would not tell us whose.
Dad was doing a naked Mom,
but the boobs fell off.

*

The Hobbyhorse

A housewarming: three glasses
in the best house in the world,
made of couch pads and cushions,
in the study, under the desk.
What fun it is to be feasting,
stooped up in the dark!
But the train of chairs is coming,
the moored bed is all set to sail.

*

Mamma

A game of chess. Silence. Dusk.
Even the black is dozing off.
Dad, is Mom your wife?
I'm in love with your wife.
I think one day I'll marry her.
A long, tender, serious look.
Night. Four-knight debut.
Pawn endgame. Linear mate.

*

March of the Tin Soldiers

They arrived with backpacks and songs,
pitched tents nearby, tore the wings off
my dragonflies, maimed my crickets,
gouged the eyes out of my baby frogs,
got on my and Grandma's nerves,
and the mess they left behind!
Still, I couldn't wait to become
a Young Pioneer.

*

The Sick Doll

A visit to a speech therapist
is boring as all hell.
With a stick in the mouth,
you can't speak very well.
The session drags on.
The clenched fist goes numb.
—Vera, you are such a moron . . .
—And you are so grrrr-ossly dumb!

*

The Doll's Burial

Presents. Toasts. Relatives. Girlfriends.
A flock of bowls flitters around the table.
Grandma, did you have a favorite toy?
Grandma, can you hear me? I can. I did.
A doll it was. A rag doll. I called her Nell.
Eyes with lashes. Pleated hair. A skirt with frills.
In nineteen twenty-one we ate her. She was
stuffed with bran. A whole cupful of bran.

*

Waltz

I'm so happy, I'm so happy:
any day now I'll start the first grade!
I've bought the prettiest elastic
and passed the poop test.
I'll be the best, I simply know it!
I can sing, play the piano, handwrite,
and I am rereading *Huckleberry Finn*
for the fourth time.

*

The New Doll

So, this is my younger bro?
Sure, I am very glad.
As a young naturalist of renown,
I'm mad about pigs newly born.
Dad keeps cracking silly quips,
Mom and Grandma skip on sleep . . .
Let him bawl, I do not mind.
Walk me to the kindergarten, Gramps!

*

Mazurka

My greatest talent is finding what has been lost.
That is why everyone needs me so much.
Only I can find what vanished, or was dropped,
stuff like beads, pins, coins, needles, paper clips.
I can find berries at night, fireflies in daylight.
I also know how to untangle Dad's fishing line,
and can touch my nose with the tip of my tongue.

*

Russian Song

Sundress, like a sail
in the cornflower sea;
cloudlets, like foam
for my sun bath;
emerald flies
on recon flights;
Dame Ladybug
and the almighty Lord.

*

The Peasant Plays the Accordion

The mother is twenty-eight,
the daughter is almost three.
We are out in the cold,
blowing bubbles of soap
to put them on a Christmas tree.
Unbelievable: they freeze
into balls, all opalescent,
with warm laughter inside.

*

Folk Song

A cigarette box for a house.
A matchbox for a limo.
Time to go, ladybug: we can't
make the groom wait!
In the garden, by the shed,
in an empty tuna tin,
we will have a modest wedding,
the June bugs might drop in.

*

Polka

My little bro, a preschooler,
came home with a dirty joke.
From that buddy of his, Azat,
you can expect the worst!
I said, "Great! Quick,
go tell it to Mom!"
Mom chuckled, blushed,
and hid behind her book.

*

Italian Song

Threaded a needle
three times for Gramps,
helped a snail
get across the road,
didn't call Dad
a wretched drunk.
Being a goody-goody
got me really tired!

*

Old French Song

They didn't let me see,
kept shooing me away,
told me not to sing,
put me up on the couch,
then a nurse came
and tapped a syringe . . .
I had a sister once.
But not for very long.

*

German Song

I don't want to be friends with Sashka:
he's stupid, arrogant, rude.
Mom, make me a bow!
The arrows I'll cut myself.
We can use a guitar string.
Did you tie it? Too slack.
He's such a braggart, you know:
tells lies, like he has a dad!

*

Neapolitan Dance Song

The water, deep and cold.
Strong current. Boggy bank.
A grown-up is someone who
never stays in till he's blue,
till pins prickle the chest, till eyes
are red, goose skin covers the legs . . .
Someone who yells from the bank:
Get out right now! But I don't hear.

*

The Nurse's Tale

Guess what me, Inna, Katia, and Rita
were doing yesterday at the playground!
We were playing the Crucifixion. I was
Jesus the Saver. They called me
all kinds of names, like "dumbhead," "idiot,"
whipped me with nettles about my legs,
beat me manually and with a stick, then
tied me to the cross with a skipping rope.

*

The Witch

A scary laughing mask,
arsenic served for six . . .
The bloodier the story,
the sounder the sleep.
A sea of innocent blood,
corpses by the score . . .
The sister shut her ears.
"More!" the brother implored.

*

Sweet Dreams

I would put on Mom's bra,
stuff it with any old things,
filched my sister's hygiene pads,
stuck them to my bare butt,
and when Mom caught me at that,
I would run away and cry.
As for putting on Mom's high-heel shoes and strutting in
    front of the mirror—
never, no way!

*

Song of the Lark

I look at the map of stars,
then at the starry sky,
and see that the stars are looking
at my map of stars, and they see
a meadow, by a river,
on the planet that is third from the sun,
some earthlings pointing
a flashlight at the map of stars.

*

The Hand Organ Man

Mommy bathed her girl,
Daddy dried her off,
Grandpa hurried with
a nightie for her,
Grandma smoothed the sheets,
brother fluffed the pad,
Mommy laid her down,
Grandpa tucked her in.

*

In Church

Serene icons. Gloomy worshippers.
A few of the former, crowds of the latter.
Dad, don't you know how to pray?
You just ask God for whatever
you want. But within reason:
not for a puppy, or for a car—
ask something easy. Like,
let no one ever die.

[breakfast]

Dad's breakfast: two eggs, sunny side up.
Mom's: one egg, hard-boiled.
Done with milking birds,
I'm busy drilling clouds.
Grandpa Rorschach, look:
aren't they simply grand?
This one's a bride, that one's a groom.
They've coupled. Now they evaporate.

[An Apollo]

An Apollo swinging an ax: my dad. So handsome!
Thick as they are, dead trees succumb to his strength
and tumble into nettles; he saws them into logs,
hauls the logs on his back, then chops them
into billets, the good-looking, powerful man that he is.
My father, aged thirty, slim, wiry, vernal!
What is history if not gossip cast in dull bronze?
The white-toothed lumberjack grumbles about the
    government.
With my sharp features and unfeminine broad shoulders
I resemble him, the bronze lumberjack. I pick up the ax
to see what I am worth. The crispy wood chips that smell
of watermelon fly in a spray left and right . . .
A lifetime ahead of us, Daughter!
Though not of noble blood, we've got a strong grip on life.

[The duckling]

The duckling was ugly, dressed in ugly clothes,
had skinny legs and a long, thin braid.
Looking nothing like a fairy-tale queen,
the duckling would loudly, arrogantly,
publicly denigrate herself.
The duckling discovered that all people were beasts,
that joy was not of this world and likely never would be.
The fear of darkness outweighed the fear of heights,
and the unhatched breasts painfully itched.

[Pain]

Pain, you are the sole proof
that my body exists.
You have made your point;
now cease. But I
will never believe
the body is all
there is to me.

[Girl-students]

Girl-students of the school of music,
we would call each other on the phone,
put the receiver on the piano, and play
the pieces we had just learned.

The receiver would tumble to the floor,
followed by the sheet music,
our parents would rage:
You're blocking the line!

But we went on playing,
making mistakes, overdoing the pedals,
giggling and cursing. We did that

not out of stubbornness, but because
you simply cannot stand
beautiful music all by yourself.

[What]

What is it?—howling, doubled up.
A burst of light. Plasma boiling.
A little big bang: the first
orgasm in my life.

[Crossing]

Crossing a meadow of daisies,
pushing the pram along
a jolty path (a tiller
behind the plow),
singing peasant-style,
I pluck a daisy: *Look!*
From the pram a pair
of wide-open eyes
stare back at me.

[No idea]

—No idea who the groom will be, but I know
what I'll be wearing: a blue-and-white gown,
sleeveless, high heels, no gloves . . .
Just for that, I am ready
to get hitched right now—
pointed breasts, the face
finely chiseled, a dull glow
in the enormous eyes . . .
—Mom, is it hard to get divorced?

[Diary]

No meetings, no poems, no books,
no quips, no funny clippings . . .
Diary, you voracious beast,
shut your trap, I have nothing
to feed you on. Except this, take it,
choke on it—something my Grandma
recalls, maybe first thing she remembers:
"It was a famine, for months and months we had
no bread at all, I have no idea what we lived on,
but for some strange reason my tiny legs were plump.
So, there I was, sitting, stroking my calves, and I said:
'Mommy, let's cut them off, cook them, and eat them.'"
Grandma often tells the story, each time we gather
at the holiday table. She laughs joyously as she tells it.

[A rickety]

A rickety fence on which:
a glass jar, a washrag, a sponge.
In vain the goldfinch clicks
its broken cigarette lighter.
Two minnows: the whole catch.
Two carrots from the veggie patch.
Mom's listening to the Beatles,
Dad, to Radio Liberty.

[ever]

ever so gently
the cradle rocks
a bumblebee naps
inside a rosebud
in a puddle the rain
fell asleep like a drunk
where is she loafing
that daughter of ours

[Rain]

Rain on the lake, a parade:
light and trim, on the water's top
tin regiments, one by one,
march in columns. A brief
downpour promises plenty
of mushrooms. Cicadas
are all for it. Huge drops
hang off the clothesline.

[Sulking]

Sulking is ugly! Instead
why don't you learn
to say THANK YOU
in every tongue that exists.
"Not bad at all: virtually
a polyglot!" the angel on duty
will say, and will turn the key.

[new]

Everything I wear is brand-new:
my reflection in every
shop window!

[To stroke]

To stroke a book's face, to eat
black currants from a bush,
to kiss the singer's hands
and the song on his mouth.
The hands smell like rain,
the song smells like milk.
Summer, slow down, stay,
don't go away!

[My male]

My male ancestors: all
tobacco and alcohol.
Seems no man in Dad's line
died in sober mind.
A teetotaler who drinks
milk for toasts, I know:
unlike the kin of my dad
I'll die sober, though maybe mad.

[Shine]

Shine, conquer, rule!
Thanks, but no thanks.
The more I like people,
the more precious is my solitude,
as I roam meadows and fields,
follow paths, half-overgrown,
and tell the clouds up above
how good all of you are!

[from the sea]

All summer winds come from the sea,
all winter snows come from mountain caps.
If you expand your soul to the limit,
you will discover: space has no bounds.

If in autumn you inhale rain and smoke,
or smell lilies of the valley in spring,
or simply wake up being loved,
you will discover: the soul has no bounds.

[sit]

sit by the river
keep pitching
your troubles in it
watch them
float away
with the current
too light
to drown

[Tears]

Tears, like a blind man's fingers
groping for cheeks, a nose,
unable to name the face:
What happened? Who is this?
The curve of a thin mouth,
the false track of a scar
(childhood, a shard of glass) . . .
Seems it is me.

[dogs]

Get 'er! Seek 'er! Go!
Yoshka, how can it be?
Death trains us, as she
takes our dogs away.
Where is the fearless pup?
Where is the cheerful pal?
And I growl, and I whimper,
and I chew on the leash . . .

[Written]

Written in the dark, by the light
from one's own eyes,
the secret lines that had taught us
how to cry. And the covenant is
so inviolable that anyone can
read those lines with no light,
with eyes shut.

[for the road]

Dad, one for the road?
Mom, more tea?
Was it good for you
when you conceived me
in the kingdom of permafrost,
in the realm of midnight noon?
Mom said: *Yes, it was.*
Dad said: *Can't recall.*

[The State]

The State sent them way up north,
and so they went, three bags in hand.
"No cursing when the girl is around!"
The inmates were mum around Mom.
One more melt, with its fire tongue.
Snowdrifts that look scorched.
Inmate of the womb, how I craved
to get out, onto the mainland!

[Down]

Down the middle, along the edge,
in the language of touch,
by the shivers, in Braille,
I will read your confession,
and with all of my skin,
with all of its nether side,
I will reply *me too*
to a birthmark, a blemish, a scar.

[An assistant]

An assistant, a plaything,
a concubine, a slave,
I reserve the sole right
to be the second to say
I love you to an artist,
a hero, a king, a beau,
and to be the first to declare
I do not love you anymore.

[All]

All the events of summer
that spring saw in her dreams,
all that in this world has been
as light to me, and all I will
see in dreams in the other world—
all that can nicely fit
under one umbrella.

[Making]

Making love as much as we wish,
skinny-dipping whenever we feel . . .
How is life, naked kids?
Life teems in every cell!
All alone, as in an Eden,
no laws, as in dreams . . .
I spread my skirt on the grass:
life of mine, come to me.

II

[A thought]

A thought is not ripe,
if it cannot be put in four lines.
A love is not ripe,
if it cannot be put in one "ah."
A poem is poorly written, if right now
I start looking for rhymes and stick to a meter.
A life has been poorly lived,
if it cannot be put in one "yes."

[So much]

So much life in me!
Enough for ten.
I must have been born
to birth ten kids
and to school each
in music.

[an ant]

an ant on the sleeve
a dragonfly on Rabelais
a man lying on grass
on earth on the Earth
on the Earth's chest
curled up asleep
don't wake him up
maybe later
not now

[I am]

I am
a nail
being driven in
while I try
to keep
straight
hoping
the carpenter
will get tired
or the hammer
will break
or the board
will crack and I
will roll
into a cozy nook
and will find you there
my love
my love

[My quill]

My quill, spare no ink,
be it black, blue, or red,
praise the day when God divided
vowels from consonants!

[And so]

And so, I accept my fate,
write rhymed odes praising it,
as you brand my brow
with red-hot iron: "beloved."

[Remember]

Remember me the way I am
this very instant: brusque and absent,
with a word beating against my cheek
like a butterfly caught in a curtain.

[Summer]

Summer, a country house,
vacation, sunshine, life,
love at its peak . . .
Bluebells, why aren't you ringing?
Belfry, sparrows, cicadas,
show them how to do it!
I feel no pain today!
And you, feeling better?

[a handful]

a handful of wild strawberries
vacation in paradise
in the book we are reading
my bookmark got ahead of yours
though neither of the two
got very far in the text
water lilies by the pier
the edge of the globe

[at twenty]

at twenty
to fuck

at thirty
to love

what will I do at forty?

will look lively
will work
will be proud:
see, straight As!

will hope
to be pardoned
at fifty

[After]

After a long-awaited love meet
sparrows in the belly tweet:
riffraff and cadgers, they know
where seeds have been spilled!

[Today]

Today, he's in a good mood,
which means the first wind
I run into will be favoring,
all news will be good,
all burdens light as air . . .
Hush, my heart, listen:
he's singing in the shower!

[Joyfully]

Joyfully, tenderly, ardently,
a spendthrift, I let myself go.
My heart is a piggy bank
you've broken to bits.
Will they last us long,
the coins strewn about,
the colorful skimpy dresses,
caresses, dreams, rhymes, tears, books, winters, years?

[Giving birth]

Giving birth was the funniest.
"Go," said the gruff nurse
and vaguely waved
in the direction down the hallway.
I grabbed my belly and went.
Kept walking and walking,
then saw a mirror, and in it a belly
dressed in a shirt up to the navel,
on thin shaky legs
the color of lilac . . .
Laughed for about five minutes.
Five minutes later gave birth.

[milky]

The milky moon, snug and comfy,
rolls in a mist, light and smoky.
Let us rattle off a prayer,
let us put the babe in the cradle.
Goats will bow to him and will go back
to their feed. But the stars know something
the astronomers never dreamed of.

[Eyeglasses]

Eyeglasses? Who needs them?
They fog up when we kiss,
rub against eyelashes,
deaden smells and sounds,
send tears off their tracks . . .
And they're no help at all when you look
for what has been lost.

[A book]

A book: a dream seen in sleep,
and a textbook on interpreting dreams.
What is better than reading?
Reading together, aloud, before sleep.
Will the salty water slake
the thirst I feel?
In my dreams, saw Pushkin twice.
Onegin, not once.

[Like]

Like a bride, I would ready my husband,
like a widow, I would see him off,
when he was gone, I knew no peace,
when he returned, I ran to embrace him,
barely alive myself. Meat and buckwheat.
Tastes good? Not too cold? More salt?
Darling, how heartless of you
to go to work every day!

[I got]

I got tanned all over
on a nameless island:
not a spot omitted,
not a single defect,
I am all like chocolate,
or fresh-brewed tea
from Sri Lanka, but
for one pale streak
under the wedding band.

[I used to be]

I used to be a lousy housewife:
for ten years I had no idea
whether the oven was
in working order.
Then I radically changed and
became a good housewife.
Now I know for certain:
the oven is not working.

[To run]

To run naked in the pouring rain,
to sleep in the garden on a cot,
tomorrow we'll go mushroom hunting,
I will find four big white ones,
you will proudly show me your catch:
three perches and two carps . . .
And, please, no forbidden fruits!
What for? If we can't, we can't.

[Can't]

Can't write? Read.
Can't read? Write.
Can't write? Write
letters. Can't write
letters? Read aloud
nursery rhymes
to your kid.

[clocks]

All the clocks are running fast.
Can't stand it anymore:
I will abandon my nestlings,
will hide in a cuckoo's nest
as the custom demands, and then,
to spite the maker of clocks,
I will leap out the window,
yelling, "Coo-coo!"

[You want]

You want them to listen to you?
To heed your instructions?
To hang on to each of your words?
To look around: What did he say?
You want that? Be an engineer
on a commuter train, tell them
in an offhand, condescending voice:
"Michurinets, next stop Vnukovo."

[It is not]

It is not at all like the flight
from Eden to hell (a kick
in the butt, and you're gone):
the Fall occurs gradually,
the way teeth fall out.
Not the fire-spitting void, but
a placid garden, a honey-sweet fruit—
why, it's paradise! But the poor sinner
cannot recognize it at point-blank range.

[lots]

lots of knives
but only one cuts
lots of pens
but only one writes
lots of men
but I love only you
maybe at last you will
sharpen the knives?

[Daddy]

Daddy, make some tea,
tell me I'm a bitch,
call me poor kid,
sit next to me . . .
So many loves in the past,
none of them the first,
none of them true,
none the only one.

Three-Leaved Mirror

1.
I look in the mirror:
there she is, the woman
loved by the man
I love, and I feel
envious and
jealous.

2.
I look in the mirror:
there she is, the woman
desired by the man
I desire, and I
close my eyes
and sigh.

3.
I look in the mirror:
there she is, the woman
whom my last man
will forsake,
and I gloat,
and grow old.

[A child]

A child is a clay piggy bank
shaped like a cat or a pig
with its back rough or smooth
and a narrow slot in the head.
Pinch by pinch, you drop in the slot
small change: musical notes, the alphabet,
hoping to crack the bank open
the day you wake up bankrupt.

22 Haiku

1

the summer menu
scribbled outdoors in chalk
washed out by the rain

2

the star of Christmas
the alpha and omega
in the Cross cluster

3

the sunflower is
one head taller than the sun
two than you and I

4

dearest first man
leftover Eden apples
the swollen belly

5

slaughter not the pig
that knows how to seek and find
precious truffles

6

I am near death
you are right next door immersed
in crossword puzzles

7

the longer I live
the vaguer is my notion
of what death might mean

8

calm on the outside
so as to hear better
the turmoil within

9

we stroll in the park
I look at little children
you look at mothers

10

a whistling teapot
the song comes into being
at the boiling point

11

naked black-skinned men
riding ebony horses
greetings to centaurs

12

a midday siesta
the wind rocks a dragonfly
resting on the swing

13

when you are alone
your letters become longer
your poems shorter

14

a red-yellow leaf
quickly scoots across the road
when the light turns green

15

stifling summer heat
a fluttering butterfly
fans the cheek like wind

16

a stone on my heart
each of the three roads from it
runs and leads to you

17

seven lying goats
a chorus line's bivouac
a brief interlude

18

old women topless
young girls wearing bathing suits
I take my top off

19

the stiletto heel
of my new shoes has pierced
a dry autumn leaf

20

lawn please forgive me
only one leaf of your grass
will be a bookmark

21

at a liturgy
in the dense crowd I do not
dare to cross myself

22

Jesus has risen
the graveyard is all littered
with colored eggshells

Dido

Life has abandoned me.
Mournful, I cannot
get warm by the fire,
only inside it.
And since I have failed
to be to the sailor a hearth,
I will be a beacon to him:
will light up a torch,
will get royally clad
as I did of old,
will undo my braids—
hair burns well.

[by now]

by now I know
there is no death
but still know not
how to bring
the news
to the dead

[Out there]

Out there, a lost kid
is crying: my childhood.
Out there, a mixed-up girl
is sobbing: my adolescence.
Out there, a harrowed fool
is weeping: my youth.
They all are in tears, they think
I have forgotten them,
they do not know that I am simply
being kept away from them,
that I am crying along with them
out here, in the future.

[on the way]

on the way to you
was writing verses about you
finished and realized
I was headed the wrong way

[In the morning]

In the morning get dressed in black,
try to pick an appropriate blouse . . .
Learn as you may to die,
funerals you will never master.
Learn as you may to grieve,
you will never know how to say
My condolences, and then to nod,
should they thank you.

[Afraid]

Afraid you will forget? Write down.
Afraid to write down? Memorize.
Afraid to memorize? Write down.
I do write down. I am afraid.

[Love]

Love: a variety of local anesthesia.
First an injection, then slaughter.
Half a life, half a memory, half a
heavenly kingdom for a half
hour with you.
On a train, in tears, in church, raving,
I beg the sly doctor: need a fix, take half
a life, half a death, half a memory, half a . . .

[wish]

Dusk. Dogs bark.
Waters, dead still.
The angler keeps nodding off.
No bites, fisherman?
A fish takes the hook,
gives it a yank:
"What's your wish, old man?"
"Not a thing."

[Who will]

Who will weep with the weeping willow,
who will mock the mockingbird,
who will dare make happy
the one who fears joy,
who will praise a sad joke,
will shield a travesty from jeers,
who will make the forget-me-not
forget how little time is left to bloom?

[sweet]

sweet it is to sleep
next to your man
after breakfast and
before dinnertime
dreams of buttercups
of sunshine in brushwood
after lovemaking
before old age

[enough]

"Why do you need the top?
You don't have anything yet!"
Grandmother. Mother. Aunt.
Each repeating it three times,
enough for me to understand:
everything means breast. Or breasts.
Many a bra I have gone through
before realizing I did have everything
then, and only then. All I have now
is a chest with a scar shaped like a star,
and fear for those I love. Nothing else.

[Babbled]

Babbled in shrubs with a pedophile,
bathed with a fetishist, with stockings on;
a lesbian rocked me gently
in her strong hirsute arms;
with a gay, I shaved my head;
whipped a masochist till he bled;
wept with an impotent one, while he was hugging me . . .
All for love, for love, all for love.

[words]

To me the orphan's tenderness,
those words, long worn out, are
what a cigarette is to a smoker
after a New York–Moscow flight.
Only thus I know who I am,
still attractive, alive . . .
After the passport check, as I wait
for the luggage to arrive.

[Without you]

Without you, my unquenchable,
my placid light,
woes are bearable,
joys are not.
Without you, my good old pal,
my gentle foe,
grief is bearable,
happiness is not.

[out there]

What will I be doing out there?
Riding the bicycle they stole.
Rereading the books they borrowed and never returned.
Necking with the boys that other girls took from me.
Fondling the aborted kids.
Stroking the hair
of those left behind,
while they fall asleep.

[Bullets]

Bullets leave a line,
a whole stanza of dots . . .
Gunman, what was it out there?
Sharpshooter, what was it out there?
A girl? A boy?

no one to write
everyone dead
no one to write to
everyone dead

[Swallows]

Swallows turned into ravens.
Beekeepers sealed the honeycombs.
Time to pay for funerals,
time to order gravestones.
Rain and wind at night
rattle the boarded windows.
Time to finish the requiems
left unfinished by the Mozarts.

eyes
icons
close
far off
a lullaby
to go
a live
tear
on a dead
cheek
the last
point
of view

[Neither]

Neither all that pretty,
nor all that plain,
prone to laughing in videos,
looking sad in mirrors,
in snapshots sharp-faced,
simple, as they claim;
many will see me in dreams
when I am no longer around.

[A perennial]

A perennial wanderer, even at home
you keep your toothbrush in a travel kit;
a perennial bachelor, after a family dinner
you wash only your set of plates;
a perennial teenager, you look at women as if
through a chink in the boards of the changing room;
a perennial boy, you leave your observation post
to go fishing on the banks of the Lethe.

[To write]

To write lines that make pages get stuck,
make eyes shut tight, make a reader
see you in dreams, make wasps cling
to a line not because its rhythm and rhymes
are sweet, but because, being light, the line rocks
like a boat, like a cradle, like a hammock
in a pine grove . . .

Here lies Vera Pavlova—
do not walk on by!—
incurably alive,
incorrigibly right.

[Homeland]

Homeland is not a landscape,
but a group portrait in an interior:
books crowding the shelf,
a crowd of shoes by the door,
literal tears and laughter,
quick and witty talk,
one song enough for all,
and Brodsky, still dead.

[I will]

I will stop by at the zoo,
will take a look at kids,
at stray dogs,
migrant geese,
at pigeons, at clouds, and,
stunned by the beauty of
a common weed, will miss
the elephant.

[To live]

To live until the end of the world,
to see with my own eyes
what it will be like: a comet,
a bomb, a volcano, or a tsunami,
to survive it, and then to depict
a tree, the sun, the sea
on the icy tablets
of nuclear winter.

[Russian]

Whispered in Russian
when conceiving me,
screamed in Russian
when birthing me,
sang in Russian
when swathing me,
were silent in Russian
when seeing me off.
No, I will never
write poems
in English.

Safety Instructions

First you, then the child?
First the child,
then your neighbor's child,
then all the other kids on the plane,
the elderly, hugging each other,
the squealing men,
the laughing women,
the frantic stewardesses,
the cursing pilots,
the lapdog in its basket,
and then you,
just before
the soft landing
on a cloud.

[tipsy]

Sweet it is, being tipsy,
to sleep on your coat
spread right on the earth.
Maybe as sweet as in it?
Peaceful is sleep in the grass.
Maybe as peaceful as under it?
His widow inherited all he had:
the house, the garden, the sky.

[The doctor]

The doctor left. Anguish came,
sat down on the bed, and
asked the old man
what he would like to be:
a monument, a ship,
a million books?
"A cook in the restaurant car on the Orient Express,"
the old man replied.

[very]

A very, very old photo:
the dress, faded and pale,
the landscape, out of vogue,
the cloudlet, worn down,
the photographer, a victim of drink,
died a terrible death.
But the face in the photo is still
very, very young!

[They]

They asked for my blessing on Skype.
Announced the engagement on Facebook.
Showed the wedding on YouTube.
The screen saver on the PC: grandkids—
a boy, and . . . another boy.
An SMS: Are you coming?—I am.
A smiley. A heart. A smiley.
Shall I buy an iPad for each?

[Scary]

Scary times? Lie down,
get some sleep.
Can't sleep alone anymore?
Lie down, get some sleep.
Not a minute for sleep?
Lie down, get some sleep.
The bedroom burned to ash?
Lie down, get some sleep.

[Night]

Night. Paris. Eyes and hands
floating in the haze of mirrors:
a young *coiffeuse* dyeing
an old woman's hair.
One reflection blissfully smiles
at the other reflection.
Both exceptionally beautiful.
Well, Paris, which one
is closer to
perfection?

[You and me]

A book on a shelf: in profile.
A book in hand: full face.
Dear book, the promised hour
has arrived, the night lamp
has been lit. You and me, alone.
Fling your pages wide open,
with all your letters
cling to me.

[ingénue]

wilted on the stalk
like a mandrake
babbled like a slender-
necked ingénue
sang the alto line
of Civil War songs
kissed the bedsheet
the one on which

[I declare]

I declare the umbrella open,
I declare the rain a sun shower,
I declare the grief forgotten,
I declare the city my home.
the past I declare as washed spick-and-span,
the future as waiting for me . . .
What do you think of such an agenda
for a dark winter day?

A Note About the Author

Vera Pavlova was born in Moscow. She is the author of twenty collections of poetry, the librettos to five operas and four cantatas, and numerous essays on musicology. Her work has been translated into twenty-two languages. She is a best-selling poet in Russia and now makes her home in Toronto.

A Note About the Translator

Steven Seymour (b. 1946) translated literary works from Polish, French, and Russian, including Vera Pavlova's *If There Is Something to Desire*. He died in 2014.

A Note on the Type

This book was set in Adobe Garamond. Designed for the Adobe Corporation by Robert Slimbach, the fonts are based on types first cut by Claude Garamond (c. 1480–1561). Garamond is believed to have followed the Venetian models, and it is to him that we owe the letter we now know as "old style."

Composed by North Market Street Graphics,
Lancaster, Pennsylvania

Printed and bound by Thomson Shore,
Dexter, Michigan

Designed by M. Kristen Bearse